LIVING WELL
WATER SAFETY

by Lucia Raatma

THE CHILD'S WORLD®
CHANHASSEN, MINNESOTA

Published in the United States of America by The Child's World®
P.O. Box 326, Chanhassen, MN 55317-0326
800-599-READ
www.childsworld.com

Subject Consultant:
Bridget Clementi, Safe
Kids Coordinator,
Children's Health
Education Center,
Milwaukee, Wisconsin

Photo Credits: Cover: Getty Images/Thinkstock; Banana Stock/Punchstock: 9-right, 25; Corbis: 8 (Michael Prince), 10, 14 (Reuters NewMedia, Inc.), 18 (Mug Shots), 19, 20, 21 (Ric Dean); Picture Quest: 5 (Photo Link/Photodisc), 7 (Corbis Images), 9 (Scott T. Baxter/Photodisc), 11 (D. Berry/Photo Link/Photodisc), 12 (Creatas), 15 (Photo 24/Brand X Pictures), 16 (elektraVision AG), 17 (Digital Vision), 22 (IVALO 140/Brand X Pictures), 25-right (Stockbyte); Punchstock: 6 (Thinkstock), 13 (Brand X Pictures), 21-right (Photodisc); Thinkstock/Picture Quest: 23, 26.

The Child's World®: Mary Berendes, Publishing Director

Editorial Directions, Inc.: E. Russell Primm, Editorial Director; Elizabeth K. Martin and Katie Marsico, Line Editors; Olivia Nellums, Editorial Assistant; Susan Hindman, Copy Editor; Susan Ashley, Proofreader; Peter Garnham, Fact Checker; Tim Griffin/IndexServ, Indexer; Elizabeth K. Martin and Matthew Messbarger, Photo Researchers and Selectors

Library of Congress Cataloging-in-Publication Data
Raatma, Lucia.
  Water safety / Lucia Raatma.
      p. cm.—(Living well)
Includes index.
Summary: Explains the importance of being safe around pools, lakes, and oceans, whether swimming or in a boat, and points out specific things one can do to remain safe in the water.
  ISBN 1-59296-090-1 (Library Bound : alk. paper)
  1. Swimming—Safety measures—Juvenile literature. 2. Aquatic sports—Safety measures—Juvenile literature. [1. Swimming—Safety measures. 2. Aquatic sports—Safety measures. 3. Safety.] I. Title. II.
Series: Living well (Child's World (Firm)
  GV838.53.S24R34 2003
  797.2'1'0289—dc21   2003006286

TABLE OF CONTENTS

CHAPTER ONE

A Day at
the Pool

Maria could hardly wait to get into her swimsuit and head to the

pool. It was a hot summer day, and she knew the cool water would

feel terrific. Before they left the house, Maria helped her mom get all

their supplies together. They put towels and T-shirts in a big bag.

"Don't forget the sunscreen," Maria reminded her mom.

Once they got to the community pool, Maria wanted to jump

right in. But first, she put on sunscreen. Then she checked to see how

deep the water was. Some little kids were in the **shallow** end, where

the water was not over their heads. Maria could go in the deep end

because she was a strong swimmer.

Lots of people were diving in the pool, so Maria stayed away from

that area as she swam. She tossed a ball with her friends, and she rested on a float for a while. When she started to get tired, Maria got out of the pool. She put on a T-shirt and shared a cool drink with her mom—some lemonade in a plastic bottle. She was thinking about getting back in, but then she heard thunder. Lightning was soon to follow.

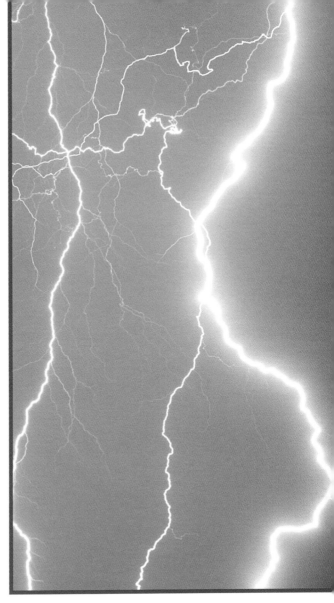

Maria was wise not to get into the pool when she realized a storm was approaching.

"Time to head home," her mother told her.

"You're right," Maria answered. "But what a great afternoon we have had!"

Swimming can be a lot of fun. Some people enjoy pools, while others like taking a dip in lakes or at the beach. But water can be **dangerous,** too. It is important to learn how to swim and to follow a few simple rules while you are near the water. Then you can stay safe—no matter where you swim.

This sign at the pool means that diving is not allowed. It is important to learn a few simple safety rules before you go swimming.

CHAPTER TWO

HOW CAN YOU STAY SAFE AT SWIMMING POOLS?

The local swimming pool is probably a favorite spot for you and your friends each summer. A dip in the pool is a welcome break from the heat. And you might like playing with a beach ball or floating on a raft. By following some simple rules, you can make your day at the pool a safe one.

Take a look at the numbers written on the walls of the pool. These tell you how deep the pool is. If you are not a strong swimmer, be sure to keep out of the deep end. Stay in the shallow

Swimming in the pool is a fun way to cool off in the summer!

Always listen to the lifeguard when you go swimming.

area where you can stand up until you improve your swimming skills.

If you do not know how to swim, stay in the shallow area. Nonswim-

mers should not go in water that is over their heads.

Whenever you are in a pool, make sure an adult is watching. You

should never swim alone. Listen to the **lifeguard,** and follow the rules at the pool. It is fun to play with your friends, but never jump on them in the pool or dunk them under the water. You could accidentally hurt each other. When you are out of the pool, walk but do not run. The area around a pool can be wet and slippery. If you run, you might fall and hurt yourself.

It is fun to use balls, noodles, inner tubes, and other toys in the water. But

You might enjoy using noodles and inner tubes in the pool, but you should never rely on them to keep you from drowning.

you should never depend on these items to keep you afloat. They could break or **deflate.** Nonswimmers should be especially careful of these floating toys. You can fall off a float or lose your grip on a noodle or ball. It is better to be a strong swimmer and rely on your skills to stay safe.

If a pool is closed, do not go swimming. A closed pool has no lifeguard. That means there is no one to help if you are drowning.

It's not safe to go swimming if a pool is closed.

This fence will prevent people from swimming in the pool when it's not safe.

Wait until the pool is open and other people are there. Pools in people's homes or yards should be protected by fences. These fences keep swimmers out when it is not safe. They also prevent small children from falling in.

CHAPTER THREE

WHAT SHOULD YOU KNOW ABOUT BOATING?

Boats can pull you while you water-ski. They can take you from one island to another. Boats can give you a place to sit while you fish. They are fun to ride in, and some can go really fast! But that is not all you should know about boats. They can flip over if you stand up in them, and they can sink if they are damaged. You should know the rules for safe boating.

The most important thing to remember is to always wear a **life jacket** when you are in a boat. Be certain it is the right size for you. Ask an adult to make sure the jacket is

Don't forget to wear a life jacket when you go boating!

approved by the U.S. Coast Guard, and check that it is free from rips or other damage. A life jacket can keep you afloat in the water. It can save your life if your boat overturns or if you fall out. Everyone should wear a life jacket, especially people who cannot swim.

Never take a boat out by yourself. Always go with

Learning about Life Jackets

Whenever you are in a boat, it is important to wear a life jacket. It will help you stay afloat if you fall in the water. Most life jackets are filled with material that floats, such as plastic foam, cork, or fiberglass. Most do not have sleeves, so you can easily move your arms while wearing one. Life jackets are sometimes called life preservers or life vests.

Even if you know how to swim, a life jacket can save you. Currents can be tricky, and even the strongest swimmer can be pulled underwater. Be smart when you go boating—wear a life jacket every time.

The America's Cup

The America's Cup is a well-known boat race. People from different countries race boats called yachts. The first yacht to win a certain number of races wins the cup.

Members of yachting teams know about water safety. They follow the rules of the race, and they keep their boats in good shape. If the weather is bad, they do not race. And they have been trained to handle emergencies.

The America's Cup trophy is the oldest award in international sports. Members of competing teams take the race very seriously. But they know how to stay safe, too.

a buddy and make sure an adult is present. Be careful getting in and out of boats. Never jump from the boat to the dock. The rules are the same for Jet Skis and canoes, as well. A small boat can be just as dangerous as a big one. Learn the right rules so you can have a safe and enjoyable time boating.

CHAPTER FOUR

How Can You Swim Safely in Lakes and Oceans?

Lakes and oceans are often exciting places to swim. Gentle waves and warm breezes can make a day in the water one to remember. But these natural areas are much different from pools. There are more things you need to remember to stay safe.

Natural areas can be great places to swim, but make sure you know a few extra safety rules.

It is sometimes hard to see the bottom of a lake or ocean. This makes it difficult to know the **depth** of the water. Ask an adult to show you how deep the water is. Then stay in the area that is shallow enough for you. The bottoms of lakes and oceans can drop sharply, and you can find yourself in over your head! If you cannot swim, be sure to stay close to the shore where the water is shallow.

Be aware of the fish and other wildlife that you are sharing the water with. Most are harmless and will leave you alone, but certain creatures, such as the jelly-

When you swim in natural areas, it's important to respect the wildlife you're sharing the water with. Most animals, such as this frog, are harmless and will leave you alone.

fish, could sting you. If you see one, tell an adult right away. No matter what you have heard, shark attacks are not common. If you think you've spotted a shark, let an adult know. But you shouldn't stay out of the ocean because you are afraid of them. You

Wearing water shoes will protect your feet while you walk along the shore.

are more likely to find seagulls and seashells than a shark.

In a lake or on a rocky beach, you may also find jagged rocks. It is always a good idea to wear water shoes to protect your feet. In oceans, pay special attention to waves. They are sometimes rough, and getting caught in a breaking wave can be scary. Learn how to judge when a

If the water isn't safe for swimming, try building a sand castle!

wave is about to break. Stay in front of or behind a breaking wave. If

the waves are too rough, get out of the water. Spend your time build-

ing a spectacular sand castle or playing catch with a beach ball.

Ocean currents can be dangerous, too. They pull you in a certain

direction, but you may not always feel yourself moving. When you enter the water, choose a nonmoving point on the beach that you can watch. This could be a flag or your mom's beach umbrella. Check this point every few minutes. If you find yourself far to one side of the point, the current may have taken you there. Wade or swim back so you are even with the point again. If you can't, get out of the water. The current may be too strong for you.

Use your mom's beach umbrella as a nonmoving point on the beach when you go swimming.

Never swim without a buddy, and always make sure a lifeguard is

watching. And never pretend to be in trouble if you are not. Faking

an **emergency** is dangerous and keeps the lifeguard from helping

others. When you go to a beach on a lake or an ocean, pay attention

to the signs that might be posted. These signs will warn you of any

dangers you may encounter or any weather conditions to be aware of.

This sign means that no lifeguard is on duty, so it may not
be safe to go swimming even if an adult is present.

CHAPTER FIVE

WHAT SHOULD YOU REMEMBER ABOUT THE WEATHER?

When it is hot and sunny, you probably love the water. A swim is the perfect answer to the heat. But remember that the sun and heat can be dangerous, too. The sun's rays can burn your skin. Always wear waterproof sunscreen to prevent this from

A day at the beach is a good way to escape the summer heat, but remember to pack waterproof sunscreen.

If you go swimming on a hot day, always drink plenty of water.

happening. Apply it before you go into the water and again after a swim. It is best to use sunscreen with an SPF (sun protection factor) of 15 or higher. Ask your parents to stock up on sunscreen before the warm weather hits.

Even if you are cooling off with a swim, take **precautions** in the heat. Drink plenty of water, and get out of the sun when you start to become too hot. Stay under an umbrella or go inside.

If you see that a thunderstorm is approaching, get out of the water! Lightning is especially dangerous around water, so don't take any chances. When the skies darken and you hear thunder, get inside

as quickly as you can. Do not stand under a tree, because trees are

often struck by lightning. Storms affect you when you are boating as

well. Pay attention to the weather reports so you can give yourself time

to get to shore before a storm hits.

Never go swimming or boating when you know a storm is approaching.

CHAPTER SIX

WHAT ELSE SHOULD YOU KNOW TO STAY SAFE IN THE WATER?

The key to staying safe in the water is learning how to swim. If you don't know how to swim, talk to your parents about taking lessons. If you are a weak swimmer, take lessons to get stronger.

You need to know what to do in case of an emergency. You might get caught in a current. Or you might get a **cramp** that keeps you from swimming well. If you feel you are in danger, call for your buddy or a lifeguard. Try to stay afloat. Then yell to get others' attention. Don't be afraid to ask for help. If a friend is in danger, tell the lifeguard right away. Trying to save your friend by yourself could be difficult. You might put yourself in danger, or your friend could accidentally pull you underwater. But maybe you can throw your friend a life ring or something else to hold on to.

You can practice good water safety by throwing your friend a life ring if he is in trouble (right). It's also important to remember your manners at water parks (above).

Never push and shove people

near water. It is too easy to fall in and

get hurt. This is especially true at water parks. Take

your turn going up the steps to the rides. Be polite and wait for others who are ahead of you. Go down slides feet first, not head first. And always listen to the lifeguards who are watching you.

It is important to drink only from plastic bottles when you are around water. Glass bottles can break and can cut bare feet. Also, never eat or chew gum while you swim. Having anything in your mouth or throat could make you choke. Another important safety rule is not to swim when it is dark. It is hard to see other objects in the water.

Leaving this glass by the pool is dangerous. If it breaks, someone might cut his or her feet.

Be careful about getting into water that is too cold. Cold water can make your muscles move slower, and that can make it hard to swim! When you get out of the water, dry off and cover up. Otherwise, you might cool off too quickly and get chilled.

Spending several hours in the water might seem like fun. But it can be tiring, too. If you start to feel tired, get out of the water. It is hard to swim well if you are exhausted. To stay safe around water, it is important not to do too much so you don't wear yourself out. Your friends may want to stay longer, but listen to your body. Don't swim longer than you should, and don't swim too far out. Pay attention to what is safe for you. Following this and other safety rules will ensure that you are able to enjoy the water for a long time to come!

Glossary

cramp (KRAMP) A cramp is a pain caused by the sudden tightening of a muscle.

currents (KUR-uhnts) Currents are the movements of water in a lake or ocean.

dangerous (DAYN-jur-uhss) Something that is dangerous is not safe and is likely to cause harm.

deflate (dih-FLATE) A raft will deflate if the air is let out of it. It will lose its shape and will no longer help you float or swim.

depth (DEPTH) Depth is a measurement of how deep something is.

emergency (i-MUR-juhn-see) An emergency is a sudden and dangerous situation. It requires immediate attention.

lifeguard (LIFE-gard) A lifeguard is a person who is trained to save swimmers who are in danger.

life jacket (LIFE JAK-ett) A life jacket is an item you wear that will keep you afloat if you fall in the water.

precautions (pri-KAW-shuhns) Precautions are actions you take to keep something dangerous from happening.

shallow (SHAL-oh) Something that is shallow is not deep.

Questions and Answers about Water Safety

I have a pool in my backyard. Is it safe to go in whenever I want?
No. You should never go in without an adult watching you.

Is it okay to swim near diving boards? No. As soon as you dive in, swim clear of that area. It is important to leave that section of the pool open for other divers.

If I go swimming in the ocean, should I worry about getting attacked by a shark? You should always be aware that you share the ocean with other creatures, but it is not likely that you will be attacked by one. Let an adult know right away if you see a shark or a jellyfish. But it is also important to pay attention to ocean currents and how deep the water is.

Is it safe to be on a boat during a thunderstorm? No. You are still on the water, and that can be dangerous if there are strong winds or lightning. If you know a storm is approaching, ask an adult on the boat to get you back to land as soon as possible.

Helping a Friend Learn about Water Safety

▸ If a friend doesn't know how to swim, encourage her to get lessons. Offer to take lessons with her, even if you already know how to swim. When she learns, swim with her often.

▸ Ask to be your friend's swimming buddy. This way, you can both look out for each other.

▸ Show your friend the rules posted at the swimming pool. Talk about what each rule means, and always listen to the lifeguard.

▸ If you are swimming and your friend seems tired, suggest another activity. Swimming is fun, but so is resting with a cool drink or building a sand castle.

Did You Know?

▸ A person can drown in less than two minutes underwater.

▸ Some people drown when they accidentally fall into a swimming pool.

▸ Fences around a pool are there for a reason. Never climb over a fence to swim when a pool is closed.

▸ Some currents can pull a swimmer under the surface of the water.

▸ The sun's rays are the most harmful between 10:00 A.M. and 4:00 P.M.

How to Learn More about Water Safety

At the Library: Nonfiction
Boelts, Maribeth. *A Kid's Guide to Staying Safe around Water.*
New York: PowerKids Press, 1997.

Carter, Kyle. *In Water.*
Vero Beach, Fla: Rourke Press, 1994.

Gutman, Bill. *Recreation Can Be Risky.*
New York: Twenty-First Century Books, 1996.

Loewen, Nancy, and Penny Dann (illustrator). *Water Safety.*
Plymouth, Minn.: The Child's World, 1997.

Neudecker, Joan, Colleen Politano, and Chris Buffett (illustrator).
Adrift! Boating Safety for Children. Merrillville, Ind.: ICS Books, 1994.

At the Library: Fiction
Davis, Gibbs, and Abby Carter (illustrator). *Camp Sink or Swim.*
New York: Random House, 1997.

Kalman, Bobbie. *A Canoe Trip.* New York: Crabtree, 1995.

On the Web
Visit our home page for lots of links about water safety:
http://www.childsworld.com/links.html

Note to Parents, Teachers, and Librarians: We routinely verify our
Web links to make sure they're safe, active sites—so encourage your
readers to check them out!

Through the Mail or by Phone

American Red Cross National Headquarters
431 18th Street, N.W.
Washington, DC 20006
202/639-3520

National Center for Injury Prevention and Control
4470 Buford Highway, N.E.
Atlanta, GA 30341
770/488-1506

National SAFE KIDS Campaign
1301 Pennsylvania Avenue, N.W.
Suite 100
Washington, DC 20004
202/662-0600

National Safety Council
1121 Spring Lake Drive
Itasca, IL 60143
630/285-1121

The Nemours Center for Children's Health Media
Alfred I. duPont Hospital for Children
1600 Rockland Road
Wilmington, DE 19803
302/651-4046

U.S. Consumer Product Safety Commission
Washington, DC 20207
800/638-2772

Index

About the Author

Lucia Raatma received her bachelor's degree in English literature from the University of South Carolina and her master's degree in cinema studies from New York University. She has written a wide range of books for young people. When she is not researching or writing, she enjoys going to movies, practicing yoga, and spending time with her husband, their daughter, and their golden retriever. She lives in New York.